T0198972

God Made You

Stefanie McGowan
Illustrations by Gennel Marie Sollano

WestBow Press books may be ordered through booksellers or by contacting:

WestBow Press
A Division of Thomas Nelson & Zondervan
1663 Liberty Drive
Bloomington, IN 47403
www.westbowpress.com
1 (866) 928-1240

ISBN: 978-1-9736-7657-7 (sc)
ISBN: 978-1-9736-7658-4 (e)

Library of Congress Control Number: 2019915696

Print information available on the last page.

WestBow Press rev. date: 11/19/2019

WestBow
PRESS
A DIVISION OF THOMAS NELSON
& ZONDERVAN

Dedicated to our precious girls:
Hannah and Hope, our gifts from Jesus.
And to all children, who are reminders
of God's goodness and His grace.

God Made You

God gave you feet to walk

And toes that wiggle.

He gave you legs to run

And a tummy to tickle!

God gave you arms to hug

And fingers to touch.

He gave you lips to kiss

And cheeks that blush!

God gave you a nose to smell

And eyes that see.

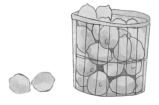

He gave you ears to hear:

"You're special to me!"

God gave you hair that grows,

And a heart that loves!

He made every detail,

You were sent from above.

Praise Jesus, the Savior,

who calls you His own.

You're special, you're perfect,

you're a reflection of His love!

God made *you*,

and you are precious to me.

I will praise thee; for I am
fearfully and wonderfully made:
marvelous are thy works;
and that my soul knoweth right well.

(Psalm 139:14)

Printed in the United States
By Bookmasters